# ARE YOU AFRAID OF THE DARK RUM?

## AND OTHER COCKTAILS FOR '90S KIDS

# ARE YOU AFRAID OF THE DARK RUM?

## AND OTHER COCKTAILS FOR '90S KIDS

### SAM SLAUGHTER

### PHOTOGRAPHY BY AMY ELLIS

Andrews McMeel
PUBLISHING®

# FOR MONICA

# TABLE OF CONTENTS

INTRODUCTION: I LOVE THE '90S    9

TOOLS    11

GLASSWARE    14

BASIC MIXING TECHNIQUES    16

CONVERTING TO METRIC    17

BUILDING YOUR BASIC BAR    17

A NOTE ON DIFFICULTY    19

RECIPES    21

     THE FRESH MINT OF BEL-AIR    22

     JUICE BOX ICED TEA    25

     ARE YOU AFRAID OF THE DARK RUM?    26

     THE TUBTHUMPER    29

     MAMBO NO. 5    30

     THE POG    32

     THE SLAMMER    33

     PICKLEODEON    35

     KIMMY GIMLET    36

     FERNETSCAPE NAVIGATOR    39

     SLIMY MARY    40

     BABY GOT BLACK LABEL    43

     JÄGERBOMBERMAN    44

     JÄGERBOMBERMAN 64    45

I SAW THE WINE — 46

I'M TOO SEXY FOR THIS GROG — 49

THE MUD DOG — 50

CRÈME RULES EVERYTHING AROUND ME — 53

NOTHING COMPARES 2 D.E.W. — 54

SEMI-CHARMED KIND OF COCKTAIL — 57

RED ROOM PUNCH — 58

I'LL NEVER LET YUZU GO, JACK — 61

BABY, I LOVE YOUR WRAY — 62

LIVIN' LA VIDA COCO — 65

AS LONG AS YOU RUM ME — 66

THE A/S/L — 69

WINDOWS 75 — 70

HOUSE OF PAINKILLER — 73

THE GIN RED LINE — 74

THE ROSSI & RACHEL — 77

POP CULTURE — 78

NOTHIN' BUT A MEAD THING — 81

WICKED GOOD BASIL COCKTAIL — 82

SAVED BY THE JELL-O — 85

GINNY IN A BOTTLE — 86

I'M THE COCKTAIL, GOTTA LOVE ME — 89

HEY ARNOLD PALMER — 90

THE RYE-U AND KEN — 93

THE BURDEN OF 90 PROOF — 94

BLUE DA BA DEE DA BA DYED — 97

DELIGHTFUL ORANGE DRINK — 98

CLEARLY CITRUS — 101

BOX OF CHOCOLATE — 102

GHOST-BUSTING JUICE                         105
ALOHA PUNCH                                 106
THE Y2K                                     109

# APPENDICES                                110

SYRUPS                                      110
INFUSIONS                                   112
PLAYLISTS                                   113
'90s DRINKING GAMES                         119

# ACKNOWLEDGMENTS                           120

# INDEX                                     122

# INTRODUCTION:

# I LOVE THE '90S

When I was a kid, I couldn't wait for Friday and Saturday and the TV shows I looked forward to all week. On Fridays, there was ABC's TGIF lineup. That meant the Tanners, the Matthews family, the Winslows, and the Fosters and Lamberts. I watched as families came together, fell apart, and then came back together to the dulcet sounds of uplifting instrumental music (or in the case of *Full House*, a number laid down by Jesse and the Rippers).

Saturday nights were much more important. If you were lucky enough to have cable at the time, you know what block of TV meant the most to '90s kids like me: Saturday Night Nickelodeon, better known as SNICK. Shows like *Clarissa Explains It All* (Melissa Joan Hart would later show up on TGIF as Sabrina the teenage witch); *The Adventures of Pete & Pete*; *The Ren & Stimpy Show* (which only about half of my friends and I were allowed to watch); my favorite, *Are You Afraid of the Dark?*; and later, *All That* and *Kenan & Kel* shaped my childhood taste and took me into angsty teenagerdom and a new century.

I bring up these two nights of television because, for me, they are the epitome of '90s nostalgia, bringing back happy memories of the comforts and fun of childhood. Now, at almost thirty and working and paying bills and doing all of those responsible grown-up things, I truly, madly, deeply miss the '90s.

This book is a booze-filled, playful attempt at getting those warm childhood feelings back.

Sure, it's not a perfect science—I can't bring back the exact feeling of my family's old burgundy couch, and I can't bring back the anticipation for the newest game for my Sega Genesis, and I surely can't bring back that weird Orbitz drink (not that I would necessarily want to)—but I'm offering something maybe better: nostalgia in a glass.

On that note, let's get to the drinks. In this book you'll find recipes for original craft cocktails that have a little fun with '90s pop culture and a selection of drinks from my childhood that I've booze-ified.

You'll also find playlists, games, and other ideas to help you plan the best '90s party since 1999 (though this time, we can feel safe in the knowledge that Y2K isn't going to destroy our entire infrastructure).

\*\*\*

Nostalgia often evokes good feelings. Cocktails often evoke good feelings. That's what this book aims to do.

# RECOMMENDED TOOLS AND GLASSWARE

Before you get started reliving the '90s, you're going to need some tools to make the drinks themselves. Below, you'll find a list of the things that are generally good to have on hand for making a variety of drinks, including all of the ones in this book. Depending on how many people you're making drinks for, having between two and four of these tools on hand is a good idea, especially in terms of the glassware, though having a second shaker handy would be smart.

*\*\*\**

# TOOLS

### A SENSE OF HUMOR

Hey, look at that. One thing down. If you've made it this far, you're in it for the long run. You're ready to conquer the Aggro Crag that is this book. All of the puns. All of the bad jokes. In this book, they're like Pringles. Once you pop, you can't stop. And by you, I mean me, and by can't stop, I mean won't stop. Semantics.

### JIGGER

Jiggers are used to measure spirits, ingredients, or your flop sweat when you realize your personal Kelly Kapowski is coming over for the first time and you desperately want to impress her. Jiggers tend to come in two sizes, each with two different measurements. The first would be two ounces and one ounce, while the second holds one and a half ounces and three-quarters of an ounce. You don't need both, but it's a good idea to have them. They're like Pokémon cards. You've gotta catch 'em all. Except there's only two, so it's pretty easy.

## SHAKERS

There are two main types of shakers out there: Boston shakers and cobbler shakers. Boston shakers consist of two parts: a large metal shaking tin and a smaller mixing glass (looks like a pint glass but is thicker). These are what you see most craft bartenders using, as shaking them looks fly and professional. If you've never shaken a drink before, I'd go for the cobbler. The Boston shaker takes a little bit of practice, and the cobbler shaker is a little more novice-friendly. It comes in three pieces—a shaker tin, a metal lid with a built-in strainer, and a cap for that lid. Simply put your ingredients in the tin, put the lid and cap on, then shake. When you're ready, pop the cap off and pour through the strainer.

## MIXING GLASS

Mixing and shaking do the same thing—they dilute and they chill. If you're working with cocktails that are *only* composed of spirits, then you're going to want to stir them. A Yarai mixing glass is a good choice, but if you don't think you'll be doing much stirring, a pint glass will do just fine.

## BARSPOON

The Stretch Armstrong of the spoon world, barspoons are long and usually have one of two things on the opposite end—a muddler (which looks like someone welded a few dimes to the end) or an icebreaker (a fat teardrop). For the purposes of this book, you probably won't be breaking much ice that way, so try to find one with a muddler on the end.

## STRAINERS

Depending on the cocktail, you're going to want to strain or even double strain it to make sure it comes out perfectly, keeping elements you don't want someone drinking in the mixing tin. Here, you'll want to get two types of strainers—a julep strainer and a Hawthorne strainer.

Julep strainers are large, bowl-looking strainers that fit into mixing glasses on an angle and allow you to get the good stuff out. Hawthorne strainers fit into mixing tins and allow you to strain from them (if you're using a cobbler shaker, you don't need one of these). If a cocktail calls for double straining, picking up a cone-shaped mesh strainer is recommended.

## BOTTLE OPENER

You can't drink with the Budweiser frogs without a bottle opener. I mean, you could, out of cans, but this is my book and my joke, so just run with it. Either way, you may need it to open juices or other ingredients.

## JUICER

For cocktails that use juice, you can go one of two ways. You can go Full 90s (never go full '90s!) and use bottled (and sometimes even sweetened—the humanity!) juices. They work just fine, don't get me wrong, but they taste different. If you can find and afford fresh fruits (lemons, limes, etc.) to juice, I recommend you do so. If you have a juicer at home already, great. If not, picking up something like the Amco enameled hand juicer is a great buy for less than twenty bucks. You simply cut the fruit in half, put the rind side up in the bowl, and squeeze. Look for one that fits lemons and limes—the bigger one that holds grapefruits isn't really necessary.

### KNIFE

You're going to have to cut citrus somehow. A good paring knife will do the trick, and you can get one for cheap just about anywhere. If you were to up your knife game, I'd also suggest a channel knife so that you can create citrus peel zests for certain cocktails.

***

# GLASSWARE

### SHOT GLASS

I feel there's no need to explain what a shot glass is. For these, I suggest heading to a Goodwill and looking for some true 1990s shot glasses. You'll know them when you see them. Neon. Shuttered theme parks. Fast-food icons in their glory days. Go for those; it'll make the drinks more authentic.

### PINT GLASS

A standard pint glass holds sixteen ounces of delicious boozy glory. Homer Simpson would be proud of you for having a few of these in your house. Beer, Bloody Marys, and more await you.

### OLD-FASHIONED (ROCKS) GLASS

Short and stubby, old-fashioned glasses are great for booze-forward drinks like the one it's named after. I imagine it's the type of glass Principal Belding hid in his desk after having to deal with those young whippersnappers from Bayside High day in and day out.

### MARTINI GLASS

Exactly what is says. You know them. Every -tini ever is served in one of these. Thin stem and a cone-shaped top. A typical martini glass holds four ounces, but they can come in many different sizes. Harness your inner *GoldenEye* and get a few of these for your drinks.

## COLLINS GLASS

Named for the Tom Collins cocktail, these are tall, thin glasses that typically hold between ten and fourteen ounces of liquid.

## COUPE GLASS

Shorter than a martini glass, coupe glasses have rounded bowls and were originally used to drink champagne. They usually hold around four ounces of liquid and look classy as f***.

## HURRICANE GLASS

Tall and looking something like a tulip, these glasses got their name for holding the hurricane, a cocktail made famous in New Orleans.

## IRISH COFFEE MUG

This heatproof glass is the best thing to use when making, well, hot drinks. You could use a regular coffee mug, but you miss out on two things: the fancy base and clear glass so you can show off your hard work.

## SNIFTER

With a short stem and a wide bowl, this type of glass is often used to serve straight brown spirits (the mouth, which is smaller than the bowl, concentrates the aromas of whatever you're drinking). Here, we'll use it for a smoked cocktail, which makes it look like a boozy, smoky snow globe.

***

# BASIC MIXING TECHNIQUES

For all of these drinks, you're going to be doing one of two things: shaking or stirring. Both are incredibly easy to do—as easy as beating the first level of Sonic the Hedgehog. While there are advanced techniques for both shaking and stirring, you won't need any of those here. (You can find them easily enough online if you're curious.) When it comes to figuring out if you need to shake or stir a drink, there are a few easy rules to follow. You stir booze-forward drinks like Manhattans and martinis. You shake drinks that have any of the following ingredients in them: juices, milk or cream, herbs, or egg whites. Shaking helps to fully integrate the various flavors in the drink.

### SHAKING

Regardless of which type of shaker you are using, the key to understanding basic shaking techniques is the direction in which you do it. After putting ice and your ingredients into your shaker, secure the lid. Once secured, hold the shaker in both hands (one on each end) and shake horizontally over your shoulder. Doing it this way— as opposed to shaking up and down—ensures that the ingredients will properly mix, dilute, and chill (the three things mixing a cocktail is meant to do).

[Optional move: Shaking your bon-bon while doing the above—a great option for parties.]

### STIRRING

Literally everything you need to know is in the word.

\*\*\*

## CONVERTING TO METRIC

Depending on where you are in the world, you might use metric units to measure your liquids. If you do, have No Fear. Below, you'll find a list of the basic conversions you'll need for the drinks in this book. While the milliliters and ounces don't line up perfectly (one ounce is technically only 29.5 milliliters), I've rounded to the nearest whole number for ease.

**.25 OUNCE - 7 MILLILITERS**

**.5 OUNCE - 15 MILLILITERS**

**.75 OUNCE - 22 MILLILITERS**

**1 OUNCE - 30 MILLILITERS**

**1.5 OUNCES - 44 MILLILITERS**

**2 OUNCES - 59 MILLILITERS**

**2.5 OUNCES - 74 MILLILITERS**

**3 OUNCES - 89 MILLILITERS**

\*\*\*

## BUILDING YOUR BASIC BAR (THINK THE BAR FROM *CHEERS,* BUT BETTER!)

For most of the cocktails in this book, you're going to be using the same few spirits. If you don't have anything in the house, here is a list of some bottles that would be helpful to have on hand. For any of these recipes, please use whatever you have in the house (or have just picked up at your liquor store). If a recipe calls for Maker's Mark and you've only got a bottle of Jim Beam hanging around, great. Use that. If I use a brand by name, it's because I think that specific type of X, Y, or Z tastes best, but your mileage may vary.

# SPIRITS

- Bourbon
- Rye whiskey
- Scotch whisky (a blended Scotch and a single malt would be ideal)
- Irish whiskey
- Brandy
- Rum (a light and a dark)
- Vodka
- Gin
- Tequila (a blanco or white tequila and a reposado or slightly aged tequila)
- Liqueurs (in the book you'll find crème de cassis, Ancho Reyes Verde, and triple sec)

# BITTERS

- Angostura bitters
- Orange bitters

There are hundreds, if not thousands, of other types of bitters available these days, so it would be a good idea to pick up a few other bottles as well. In this book, you'll see black walnut bitters and vanilla bitters used, both of which go really well in a number of cocktails.

\*\*\*

## A NOTE ON DIFFICULTY

On this week's invention exchange—cocktails! Thankfully, though, you don't have to be Joel or Mike from *Mystery Science Theater 3000* to be able to make these drinks. You don't even need to be a bartender to make these drinks. I wrote these recipes for anyone, even if the most difficult drink you've ever poured is a glass of water. That said, I also didn't want to bore those who have spent time behind the stick, so I've mixed in ingredients and flavor combinations that I hope will appeal across the board. For any of the drinks that feature infusions or syrups, you can find those recipes at the back of the book. You won't need any special tools to make them—just the ingredients listed, a jar or bottle, and a little bit of time.

# RECIPES

From riffs on classics like the Negroni ("The Gin Red Line") and the whiskey sour ("Baby Got Black Label") to original creations born from many hours talking with bartenders about ingredients and going all *Dexter's Laboratory* on my liquor cabinet ("Fernetscape Navigator," "Are You Afraid of the Dark Rum?") to grown-up versions of the kids' drinks I enjoyed at the time, these cocktails are distinctly modern sips inspired by my favorite decade.

While there is a wide range of ingredients here (even though boy bands worked with five members, sometimes you have to expand your bar beyond five bottles), all of the drinks still follow the same basic principles—to get a tasty drink, add the ingredients together and shake or stir.

# THE FRESH MINT OF BEL-AIR

2 STRAWBERRIES

2 OUNCES BOMBAY SAPPHIRE GIN

.75 OUNCE SIMPLE SYRUP (SEE PAGE 110)

.75 OUNCE LIME JUICE

ICE-COLD PROSECCO

MINT LEAF, FOR GARNISH

Now this is a story all about how this cocktail got flipped turned upside down. And I'd like to take a minute just sit right there and I'll tell you all about how to make The Fresh Mint of Bel-Air. In Bloomfield, New Jersey, born and raised, in a shaker is where it spent most of its days. Chillin' out, mixin' up, dilutin' all cool, shaking some citrus, not making a mule . . . you get the idea.

**METHOD:** Muddle the strawberries in the bottom of a cocktail shaker. Add the gin, simple syrup, and lime juice, and shake. Double strain into a coupe glass and top with the prosecco. Put a mint leaf between your palms and slap 'em together. Use the mint leaf to garnish.

The house used in the TV show *The Fresh Prince of Bel-Air* was actually located in Brentwood, not Bel-Air.

# JUICE BOX ICED TEA

**2 OUNCES BOURBON**

**.5 OUNCE LIMONCELLO**

**.25 OUNCE SIMPLE SYRUP (SEE PAGE 110)**

**ORANGE BITTERS**

**LEMON SLICE, FOR GARNISH**

I knew I hit the jackpot when I got a Ssips Iced Tea for lunch when I was a kid. These were my absolute favorite. The mix of almost-iced-tea flavor, lemon, and of course, lots of sugar was just what I needed to get through the doldrums of the school day. Sure, that energy was just a sugar rush, but I'm fairly certain, thanks to packaged foods, that most of us spent at least half of the '90s riding a sugar high. Using bourbon as the backbone for this drink, you'll still get the lemony, sugary flavor you would in the original but with significantly less sugar.

**METHOD:** Add the bourbon, limoncello, simple syrup, and bitters to a mixing glass with ice and stir well. Strain into a rocks glass with a large ice cube in it. Garnish with the lemon slice. If you've got any extra tiny straws lying around, feel free to sip through that.

# ARE YOU AFRAID OF THE DARK RUM?

**2 OUNCES SAILOR JERRY SPICED RUM**

**.5 OUNCE DARK RUM (I PREFER MOUNT GAY 1703 DARK RUM)**

**.25 OUNCE CHERRY HEERING**

**2 TO 3 DASHES WALNUT BITTERS**

**CINNAMON STICK**

As a kid, *Are You Afraid of the Dark?* was one of the best parts of weekend television. It was scary, but not too scary, and entertaining without giving you nightmares. Even though it isn't as frightening on rewatching (it's more of a comedy when you consider what kids wore back then), some episodes, like "The Tale of the Pinball Wizard" or "The Tale of the Ghastly Grinner," are still classic. I wanted a cocktail that paid homage to the Midnight Society, and that was how this drink was born. To get the full effect, you will need a smoke gun, which you can find online for under $100.

**METHOD:** Add the spiced rum, dark rum, Heering, and bitters to a brandy snifter with a large ball of ice. Stir. Next, place a piece of the cinnamon stick in your smoke gun. If you have a large glass bell (like you see on cake presentation platters), place it over the snifter, leaving a little space at the bottom to slide in the smoke gun tube. If you don't have a glass bell, anything that will hold in the smoke will do (even a coaster). Smoke for approximately 20 seconds. Keep under the bell or keep the coaster on as you serve.

**TIP:** If you don't have a smoker—or don't want to pick one up for just one drink—I recommend using Traeger's Smoked Simple Syrup. Liquid smoke is an option, too, but keep it as a last resort.

# THE TUBTHUMPER

**1 OUNCE WHISKEY (PREFERABLY IRISH), CHILLED**

**1 OUNCE VODKA (GRAIN BASED), CHILLED**

**3 OUNCES BRITISH LAGER, CHILLED**

**3 OUNCES DRY BRITISH CIDER, CHILLED**

Inspired by the anarchists that managed to find global fame with their one-hit wonder, this rousing cocktail is equal parts getting knocked down and getting up again. (Note: I don't actually support anarchists, but when they put eyeliner on and sing about drinking, you can't help but cheer for them a *little bit*.) Think of this as a British Long Island Iced Tea. Serve it with the intention that it's either a) going to be a long night or b) it's rally time and you need something to revive you. The drier you manage to find the lager and cider, the better these ingredients will go together.

**METHOD:** Pour the whiskey and vodka into a Collins glass first, followed by the lager and cider. To make it a longer drink, switch to a pint glass and add ice, though who really wants lager and ice together?

# MAMBO NO. 5

**1 OUNCE LIGHT RUM**

**1 OUNCE DARK RUM**

**1 OUNCE BLANCO TEQUILA**

**2.5 OUNCES PINEAPPLE JUICE**

**2 OUNCES ORANGE JUICE**

**SPLASH OF CLUB SODA**

**.5 OUNCE GRENADINE**

**.25 OUNCE OVERPROOF RUM**

**ORANGE SLICE, FOR GARNISH**

**MARASCHINO CHERRY, FOR GARNISH**

Like Lou Bega's coterie of ladies, this drink contains a bunch of different tastes which, when floated correctly, allows you to work your way through the flavors before everything inevitably becomes blurred together.

**METHOD:** Combine the rums, tequila, and pineapple and orange juices with ice in a shaker. Shake and strain into a pint glass filled with ice. Top with the club soda. Stir. Float the grenadine on top, followed by the overproof rum. Garnish with the orange slice and maraschino cherry.

Lou Bega's version of "Mambo No. 5" is a remake of a 1949 instrumental song by Pérez Prado.

# THE POG

**1.5 OUNCES PINEAPPLE JUICE**

**1.5 OUNCES ORANGE JUICE**

**1.5 OUNCES GUAVA NECTAR**

**1.5 OUNCES WHITE RUM**

**.25 OUNCE OVERPROOF RUM**

While I was in Hawaii, I learned about a juice drink that is commonly served around the islands—P.O.G.— a mixture of passionfruit, orange, and guava juices. Not only is it delicious but, I mean, how could that name NOT inspire a cocktail that reminds me of countless hours (OK, not really countless) slamming metal discs into those dumb little circles of cardboard? I switched out the passionfruit for pineapple in this drink (and in The Slammer, at right) because I felt it'd give you higher odds of winning your next throwdown.

**METHOD:** Shake the pineapple and orange juices, guava nectar, and white rum together with ice. Strain into a tall glass with crushed ice. Float the overproof rum on top. Serve with a side of regret for wasting time and money on cardboard circles.

**?** The name POG is derived from a brand of the juice mentioned above while the game itself, which is also called "milk caps," can be traced back to 1920s and 1930s Hawaii. If you want to go back even further, some say the game can be traced to the Japanese card game Menko, which has been played since the seventeenth century.

# THE SLAMMER

**1 OUNCE WHITE RUM**

**.25 OUNCE PINEAPPLE JUICE**

**.25 OUNCE ORANGE JUICE**

**.25 OUNCE GUAVA NECTAR**

We can't have a pog without a slammer. That'd be like having Ren without Stimpy or Milli without Vanilli. The recipe essentially stays the same, but smaller. And, of course, you throw it down your throat like you're playing for keeps.

**METHOD:** Add all of the ingredients to a shaker with ice and shake well. Strain into a tall shot glass.

# PICKLEODEON

**2.5 OUNCES BLACK PEPPER-INFUSED WHISKEY (SEE PAGE 112)**

**1 OUNCE DILL PICKLE JUICE**

**BABY DILL PICKLE OR PICKLE SLICE, FOR GARNISH**

There was no more iconic network for most '90s kids than Nickelodeon. From *Rugrats*, *Ren & Stimpy*, and *Nick Arcade* to *The Wild Thornberrys* and *All That*, Nickelodeon was the visual lifeline of our childhoods. This drink is strong and salty, just like my memories of trying and failing to impress Summer Sanders enough to get me on *Figure It Out*.

**METHOD:** Shake the whiskey and pickle juice together and strain into a martini glass. Garnish with the baby dill pickle or pickle slice (the whole baby dill will give more of a crunch).

**TIP:** Want to do this like a shot? Just keep the whiskey and the juice separate (and cut the whiskey back to 2 ounces). Drink the whiskey and follow it up with the pickle juice.

# KIMMY GIMLET

**2 OUNCES
LAVENDER-INFUSED
GIN (SEE PAGE 113)**

**.5 OUNCE FRESH
LIME JUICE**

**.25 OUNCE
SIMPLE SYRUP
(SEE PAGE 110)**

**LAVENDER SPRIG
OR LIME SLICE,
FOR GARNISH**

When you think of the phrase "girl next door," *Full House*'s pesky neighbor Kimmy Gibbler isn't usually who comes to mind, but the Gibbler was D.J. Tanner's best friend and an integral part of the show. This cocktail, like the Gibbler herself, is an essential . . . just jazzed up a little bit. The lavender infusion brings out nice floral notes in the gin that contrast quite well with the lime and simple syrup.

**METHOD:** Mix the gin, lime juice, and simple syrup together with ice and strain into a chilled coupe glass. Garnish with a sprig of lavender or a lime slice.

**TIP:** Some gimlets call for sweetened lime juice (such as Rose's brand) as opposed to fresh lime and simple syrup. You do you. A search of gimlet recipes online reveals every iteration possible, so work with what you've got.

# FERNETSCAPE NAVIGATOR

**BARSPOON OF SCOTCH WHISKY**

**1.5 OUNCES FERNET-BRANCA**

**.5 OUNCE DOLIN ROUGE**

**.25 OUNCE GRAND MARNIER**

**ORANGE PEEL, FOR GARNISH**

**MARASCHINO CHERRY, FOR GARNISH**

Ah, Netscape Navigator—we hated you, we couldn't get enough of you. If we had known things like Google Chrome would be on the horizon, we probably would've left you long before we did; but hey, in the bad ol' days, we had to use what we had. For this drink, I use Fernet—the bartender's handshake—as the backbone. This one is deep, dark, and can unlock new worlds if you have enough of it.

**METHOD:** Take a chilled coupe glass and place the Scotch in it. Swirl it around to coat and pour out the rest. Set aside. In a mixing glass stir the Fernet-Branca, Dolin Rouge, and Grand Marnier with a large ice cube until well chilled. Strain into the coupe glass and garnish with the orange peel and maraschino cherry. Bonus points if you want to hold a lit match to the peel to express the orange oils onto the top of the drink.

# SLIMY MARY

**2 OUNCES VODKA**

**.75 OUNCE CYNAR**

**1 LARGE GREEN TOMATO, CHOPPED**

**.5 OUNCE DILL PICKLE JUICE**

**.5 OUNCE LIME JUICE**

**3 DASHES WORCESTERSHIRE SAUCE**

**2 DRIED SNACK-SIZE SEAWEED SHEETS**

**BLACK PEPPER**

**WASABI (OPTIONAL)**

There were a lot of green, gloopy things that could get all over you in the nineties. Ghosts that hadn't been captured with a vacuum strapped to your back could cover you with gooey, green ectoplasm, and if you were on a Nick show and you did something bad—or even if you didn't, it really didn't matter—you got slimed. With gallons of the stuff. This take on a Bloody Mary is as full of green things as some lucky kid's hair after a physical challenge on *Double Dare*.

**METHOD:** In a blender, add all of the ingredients except for one of the seaweed sheets. Pulse until the tomato is completely blended. Double strain into a shaker with ice and shake well (if you don't strain, you'll be left with all the tomato pulp, which you don't want). Strain into a Collins glass filled with ice. Using a pair of scissors, cut a slit in the remaining seaweed sheet (be careful, as they're fragile) and slide onto the rim of the glass. While you can dump this on someone's head, it's much better when consumed.

# JÄGERBOMBERMAN 64

**1 OUNCE JÄGERMEISTER**

**.5 OUNCE ANCHO REYES VERDE**

**3 OUNCES PINEAPPLE JUICE**

**.5 OUNCE LIME JUICE**

**CLUB SODA, TO FILL**

**LIME TWIST, FOR GARNISH**

Same deal as over there, but in 3-D! I really like the combination of Jägermeister and chile liqueur, and the citrus from the pineapple helps bring all of the flavors together. While it may seem like absolutely nothing would go with Jägermeister, the fact that it's made with fifty-six different ingredients actually makes it pretty easy to work with.

**METHOD:** In a shaker, combine the Jägermeister, Ancho Reyes Verde, and the pineapple and lime juices. Shake well. In a hurricane glass, add crushed ice. Strain the drink into the glass and top with the club soda. Garnish with the lime twist.

# I SAW THE WINE

1 BOTTLE RED,
RED WINE (FIND
ONE THAT STAYS
CLOSE TO YOU,
LIKE A SPANISH
TEMPRANILLO)

.5 CUP BRANDY

5 OUNCES TRIPLE
SEC

3 OUNCES LIME
JUICE

CLUB SODA
(OPTIONAL)

6 TO 8
ORANGE WEDGES
(1 WHOLE ORANGE)

8 TO 10
APPLE SLICES
(1 WHOLE APPLE)

.5 CUP BLUEBERRIES

LIME WEDGE,
FOR GARNISH

If you see the wine, this drink will open your eyes (after two or three, it'll also drag you up to where you belong). Punches and sangrias like this are perfect for parties, because once they are batched, it's easy for anyone to pour themselves a cup. Another great thing is that you can personalize it as you see fit. If you have other fruits in the house, feel free to use them in place of what's listed below. Ace of Base may have been happy living without you, but you will not be happy living without this sangria in your life.

**METHOD:** Combine all of the ingredients in a punch bowl. Stir to incorporate. When serving, add ice to the cup. Garnish with the lime wedge.

For their song "C.R.E.A.M.," the Wu-Tang Clan sampled the 1967 song "As Long As I've Got You" by the Charmels.

# CRÈME RULES EVERYTHING AROUND ME

**1.5 OUNCES VODKA**

**1.5 OUNCES CRÈME DE CACAO**

**.5 OUNCE REPOSADO TEQUILA**

**ORANGE SLICE**

**GRATED CINNAMON**

This cocktail ain't nothing to f*** with. For this drink, I went with crème de cacao, which I think is highly underrated. What you get is a pretty tasty chocolate martini that is only bolstered by the cooked agave notes in the reposado tequila. The cinnamon-dusted orange slice garnish further heightens all of the delicious flavors in the drink. It's a simple drink but one that is flavor, flavor-full, y'all.

**METHOD:** Add the vodka, crème de cacao, and tequila to a cocktail shaker with ice and shake well. Strain into a coupe glass. Dust the orange slice with a little grated cinnamon and float on the drink.

# NOTHING COMPARES 2 D.E.W.

**2 OUNCES TULLAMORE D.E.W. IRISH WHISKEY**

**1 OUNCE BIANCO VERMOUTH (SWEET WHITE VERMOUTH)**

**.5 OUNCE MONTENEGRO**

**2 TO 3 DASHES ORANGE BITTERS**

**.25 OUNCE CRÈME DE CASSIS**

For this cocktail, I wanted something sweet and sensuous. The crème de cassis floater gives hints of black currant flavors and just a hint of purple—a color I associate with "Nothing Compares 2 U," which was written by his purple highness, Prince. The choice for Tullamore D.E.W.—beyond the easy wordplay—was that it was the first Irish whiskey I could say I truly understood and so, therefore, nothing can quite compare 2 it 4 me.

**METHOD:** Add the whiskey, vermouth, Montenegro, and bitters to a mixing glass and stir with ice. Strain into a coupe glass and float the crème de cassis on top.

# SEMI-CHARMED KIND OF COCKTAIL

**5 MINT LEAVES**

**.25 OUNCE SIMPLE SYRUP (SEE PAGE 110)**

**1.5 OUNCES WHITE RUM**

**1 OUNCE POMEGRANATE JUICE**

**.5 OUNCE LIME JUICE**

**POWDERED SUGAR, FOR GARNISH**

I'm going to go ahead and say it—this is the most iconic pop rock song of the '90s. It's become an instant sing-along jam in any bar, joining the ranks of "Sweet Caroline," "Don't Stop Believin'," or "Livin' on a Prayer." When I think of the song, I think of those red panties—they passed the test, after all. The pomegranate here gives us that nice red color. You can also turn this into a modified mojito by using a Collins glass and crushed ice.

**METHOD:** Muddle the mint leaves in the bottom of a cocktail shaker with the simple syrup. Add the rum, pomegranate and lime juices, and ice. Shake well and double strain into a coupe glass. Garnish with a "bump" of powdered sugar.

# RED ROOM PUNCH

**1 CUP WHITE SUGAR**

**4 LIMES, PEELED, PEELS RESERVED**

**4 CUPS HIBISCUS TEA, PREPARED HOT**

**3 CUPS RUM**

**1 CUP COGNAC**

**.5 CUP LEMON JUICE**

**.5 CUP LIME JUICE**

**.5 CUP CHERRY BRANDY**

What was going on in the town of Twin Peaks? What ended up happening to Agent Dale Cooper? And what the hell was going on in the Red Room? The mystery that David Lynch infused into every scene is like what you'll get in this drink. This deceptively boozy punch is not what it seems. Heavy on the spirits, too many cups of this and you're going to feel like you, too, will never escape from the Black Lodge.

**METHOD:** The morning before making the punch, take a Bundt cake pan, fill with water, and freeze for later. The next day, add the sugar and lime peels to a large bowl and mash together to release the citrus oils into the sugar. Allow mixture to infuse for between 30 and 45 minutes. Take the peels out and dissolve the sugar mixture with the hot tea. Add the rum, cognac, lemon and lime juices, and cherry brandy. Mix and add the ice block to the mixture. Garnish with the remaining lime wheels.

**?** For the lines said by *Twin Peaks* characters in the Red Room, the actors had to learn to say their lines backward. Once they were said backward, the already backward lines were then played backward.

The movie *Titanic* cost more than the actual Titanic. Adjusting for inflation, the real Titanic cost $7.5 million to build. The movie? $200 million.

# I'LL NEVER LET YUZU GO, JACK

.5 TEASPOON
CASTER SUGAR

3 DASHES YUZU
BITTERS

A FEW DROPS OF
WATER

2 OUNCES
GLEN MORAY
CHARDONNAY
CASK FINISH
SCOTCH WHISKY

LEMON PEEL

For a cocktail inspired by the movie *Titanic*, I wanted something fancy-feeling. Something timeless. This modified old-fashioned features a Scotch whisky that's been finished in chardonnay barrels, giving it a light character. Mix that with the lively, citrusy yuzu bitters and you've got a drink that is as bright and sparkling as the Heart of the Ocean diamond.

**METHOD:** Muddle the sugar, bitters, and water in the bottom of an old-fashioned glass. Add the Scotch and a mini iceberg. Express the lemon peel over the drink by gripping the peel toward the center with both thumbs and forefingers, turning the outside to face the drink, and squeezing. Rub the peel around the rim, and drop in.

# BABY, I LOVE YOUR WRAY

**1.5 OUNCES APPLETON ESTATE RUM**

**1 OUNCE WRAY & NEPHEW OVERPROOF RUM**

**2 OUNCES PINEAPPLE JUICE**

**.5 OUNCE LIME JUICE**

**.25 OUNCE ORGEAT**

**LIME SLICE, FOR GARNISH**

This song got a lot of play on our local radio station, Z100, thanks to *Reality Bites* (we're talking the Big Mountain version here, not the original Peter Frampton track). You couldn't, and still can't, help but bop your head along to the cool reggae groove. (Go ahead, put it on and try. I dare you. I'll wait.) This drink reflects that laid-back feeling with a tiki inspiration. It goes down smooth and is full of love (and by love, I mean rum).

**METHOD:** Add the rums, pineapple and lime juices, and orgeat to a shaker with ice and shake well. Strain into a Collins glass filled with ice and garnish with the lime slice.

**TIP:** Orgeat (pronounced *or-zha*) is an almond-flavored syrup that is an essential ingredient to many tiki cocktails. While you can make your own, you can just as easily buy some. I recommend Small Hand Foods brand, because it doesn't use artificial almond flavor.

# LIVIN' LA VIDA COCO

2 OUNCES MEAD

1.5 OUNCES SPICED RUM

2 TO 3 DASHES ORANGE BITTERS

COCONUT SPARKLING WATER

PINEAPPLE RING, FOR GARNISH

MARASCHINO CHERRY, FOR GARNISH

Ricky Martin was truly living the crazy life back in 1999, and this cocktail is sexy and vibrant like his megahit and *TRL* mainstay, "Livin' la Vida Loca." For this drink, I wanted something sweet with a little spice and plenty of pop. Basically, something that'll make you shake your bon-bon.

**METHOD:** Shake the mead, rum, and bitters together with ice. Pour the mixture into an old-fashioned glass filled with ice. Top with the coconut sparkling water and garnish with the pineapple ring and maraschino cherry.

# AS LONG AS YOU RUM ME

**1.5 OUNCES AGED RUM**

**2.5 OUNCES GRAPEFRUIT JUICE**

**.5 OUNCE CINNAMON SYRUP (SEE PAGE 111)**

**RHUBARB BITTERS**

**1 GRAPEFRUIT PEEL**

**GRATED CINNAMON**

Give me control of the music at any party and I'm going to put one thing on: '90s music, usually boy bands. Ninety percent of the time, someone at the party knows their choreography and with enough plying (with cocktails like these, of course), you'll be getting everybody to rock their bodies in short order. I love how grapefruit and cinnamon go together and, with the addition of rum, this drink is the sort of sipper that quickly turns into a gulper that quickly turns into an "Oh man, I need another."

**METHOD:** Add the rum, grapefruit juice, cinnamon syrup, and bitters to a shaker with ice. Shake well and strain into a rocks glass with ice. Express the grapefruit peel over the top, drop in, and then top with the grated cinnamon.

# THE A/S/L

.75 OUNCE APEROL

.75 OUNCE SCOTCH WHISKY

.75 OUNCE LUXARDO MARASCHINO LIQUEUR

ORANGE TWIST, FOR GARNISH

If you had AOL as a kid, more than likely you spent time in chat rooms (here's looking at you, AOL Kids Only Chat), talking with strangers who may or may not have given you their actual age, sex, and location. This cocktail doesn't capture the essence of those, um, uninformed choices, but it does showcase those three letters that popped up every single time a new person entered a chat room.

**METHOD:** Combine all of the ingredients and shake with cubed ice. Strain into a chilled cocktail glass and serve. Garnish with the orange twist.

# WINDOWS 75

**1 OUNCE GIN**

**.25 OUNCE LEMON JUICE**

**2 DASHES LAVENDER BITTERS**

**BRUT CHAMPAGNE, TO FILL**

**LEMON PEEL**

I was eight when my family got Windows 95, and I loved playing that free pinball game for hours and hours. I think of that time fondly, just as I think fondly of the classic cocktail French 75. I love French 75s. Like, love them. I'm talking Cory-and-Topanga love. Here, I've played with it a little bit by adding lavender bitters to give a nice floral character. I suggest using a London dry gin for this, but that's really up to you. If you can't find or don't have lavender bitters, a sprig of lavender dropped in will do the trick.

**METHOD:** Add the gin, lemon juice, and bitters to a champagne flute. Top with the champagne. Drop the lemon peel into the glass to garnish.

Ambient musician Brian Eno was the man responsible for creating Windows 95's startup sound.

# HOUSE OF PAINKILLER

**2 OUNCES DARK RUM**

**4 OUNCES PINEAPPLE JUICE**

**2 OUNCES ORANGE JUICE**

**1 OUNCE CREAM OF COCONUT**

**GRATED NUTMEG, FOR GARNISH**

**MARASCHINO CHERRY, FOR GARNISH**

This drink will make you want to jump around. Jump, jump, jump around. Full of tropical flavors and enough rum to make you want to get up, stand up, and (go on) throw your hands up, this drink, like the song, is a classic.

**METHOD:** Pack the rum, pineapple and orange juices, and cream of coconut into a shaker with ice and shake well (shaking can be accomplished by jumping around, but unless you've got mad skills, you might end up with more drink on you than the Bible's got Psalms). Strain into a hurricane glass filled with crushed ice. Garnish with the grated nutmeg and maraschino cherry. Serve like John McEnroe.

**TIP:** When it comes to painkillers, the original was created by Pusser's Rum on the island of Jost Van Dyke in the British Virgin Islands in the 1970s. If you've got access to Pusser's, great! Use it. If you don't, any dark rum will do.

# THE GIN RED LINE

**1 OUNCE GIN**

**1 OUNCE CAMPARI**

**1 OUNCE SWEET RED VERMOUTH**

**SODA, TO FILL**

This drink is basically a Negroni, but . . . well, thinner. After all, they didn't call the movie The Fat Red Blob. A classic war movie deserves a classic drink, and these two just seemed to go together. If you look at the cast of the movie, it reads like a who's who of greats—just like the ingredients in a Negroni. For the purposes of this book, George Clooney is the gin, Woody Harrelson is the Campari, and John Cusack is the vermouth. For the soda, we'll include every other major name associated with this movie (Nolte, Leto, Reilly, Caviezel, and . . . and . . . and). Basically, because you have this drink, nothing can touch you.

**METHOD:** Add the gin, Campari, and vermouth to a mixing glass and stir with ice. Strain into a Collins glass filled with ice and top with the soda. Get ready to face the line between the sane and the mad, the living and the dead.

**?** Bonus points if you get to drink this with a monkey named Marcel. Just don't give the monkey any—that'd be irresponsible.

# THE ROSSI & RACHEL

**1 TO 1.5 OUNCES MEZCAL**

**1 TO 1.5 OUNCES SWEET RED VERMOUTH**

**ORANGE WEDGE**

Together. Apart. Together. Apart. Some like Ross and Rachel together, some prefer them apart. Wherever you fall on one of the '90s greatest debates (joining "What are they really saying at the beginning of 'Circle of Life'?" and "Who is better, Britney or Christina?"), we've got a drink for you. These can be mixed together or they can be kept separate and taken as shots. It's not scientifically proven that this will taste better if you drink it on an orange couch, but this is a book about pop culture, not science, so this drink will taste better if you drink it on an orange couch.

**OPTION 1:** Clap four times with your friends, none of whom can get the rhythm right. Pour the mezcal and vermouth into separate shot glasses using one-ounce pours. Take the mezcal shot, eat the orange wedge, then follow with the vermouth.

**OPTION 2:** Using the one-and-a-half-ounce pours, add to a mixing glass and stir together with ice. Strain into a coupe glass and garnish with an orange wedge.

# POP CULTURE

**1.5 OUNCES BLANCO TEQUILA**

**2 OUNCES GRAPEFRUIT JUICE**

**.75 OUNCE LIME JUICE**

**POP ROCKS**

**HONEY, FOR RIMMING THE GLASS**

Is there a candy more fun than Pop Rocks? (The answer is no, though Fun Dip gives it a run for its money.) You can't help but smile when you put some Pop Rocks in your mouth. You can't eat them too quickly— too many at a time means the pops won't be as loud and annoying for as long—but too slowly or too few at a time and your pops might be overshadowed by ambient noise. There is an art and a technique to the perfect pop, just as there is to preparing this drink. For this one, you're going to have to work quickly. The Pop Rocks will start popping as soon as they come into contact with the honey, so you'll want to make sure everything is prepped, then work through the instructions speedily.

**METHOD:** Add the tequila and grapefruit and lime juices to a shaker. On one plate, pour your Pop Rocks. On another pour some honey. Gently dip a martini glass into the honey. Turn over and clean up the outside if any honey begins to drip (a Q-tip is great for this). Next, dip the glass in the Pop Rocks to coat the rim. Add ice to the cocktail shaker, shake well, and strain into the glass.

Mikey from Life cereal commercial fame didn't actually die from mixing a six-pack of Pop Rocks with a six-pack of Coke.

# NOTHIN' BUT A MEAD THING

**2 OUNCES SPICED MEAD**

**1 OUNCE BOURBON**

**.5 OUNCE CHERRY HEERING (OR CHERRY BRANDY)**

**2 TO 3 DASHES VANILLA BITTERS**

This cocktail is ready to make an entrance, so back on up. This drink uses bourbon to bring out the baking spice notes in both the bourbon and the mead, with the sweetness from the Cherry Heering and the bittersweet vanilla bitters to round the flavors out.

**METHOD:** Add all of the ingredients to a mixing glass with ice. Stir and strain into a coupe glass.

**TIP:** In today's craft world, it should be pretty easy to find a spiced mead. If you can't but can find regular mead, add .25 ounce cinnamon syrup (see page 111) to the regular mead for a rough approximation.

# WICKED GOOD
# BASIL COCKTAIL

**6 LARGE BASIL LEAVES**

**1.5 OUNCES DRY GIN**

**3 OUNCES PINEAPPLE JUICE**

**.5 OUNCE LIME JUICE**

Nineties slang was a hella weird thing. If something wasn't da bomb or dank, it was oogly. Or, worse, triflin'. Sometimes things were all that and a bag of chips, and sometimes they were just aight. Mad people got jiggy wit it in ways that were off the heezy. If you disagree with me, you can eat my shorts. This drink, I'd say, is the shiznit. The herbal notes from the basil and the dry gin go really well with the citrus notes from the pineapple and lime juices. Basically, it's pretty bangin'.

**METHOD:** Muddle three basil leaves in the bottom of a shaker. Add ice and the gin and pineapple and lime juices. Shake well and strain into a rocks glass with ice. Garnish with the remaining basil.

# SAVED BY THE JELL-O

**1 JELL-O PACKET**

**1 CUP BOILING WATER**

**.5 CUP COLD WATER**

**.5 CUP ALCOHOL (SEE BELOW)**

Oh, Kelly Kapowski. You were perfection. For these Jell-O shots, you can, if you want, use gelatin and whatever flavors you want, but seeing as the Saved by the Bell kids were in high school, it seems appropriate to simply use flavored Jell-O packets and modify the shots from there.

**METHOD:** Follow the directions on the Jell-O packet, substituting alcohol for half of the cold water. Pour into small cups and chill until ready.

**TIP:** You can customize your Jell-O shots by modifying the flavor of the Jell-O and/or the flavor of the alcohol you use. Here are some options:

**The Screech:** lime Jell-O/blanco tequila
**The Zack Morris:** cherry Jell-O/orange rum
**The Kelly Kapowski:** strawberry Jell-O/raspberry vodka
**The Principal Belding:** lemon Jell-O/white whiskey ("moonshine")

# GINNY IN A BOTTLE

**1.5 OUNCES GIN**

**2 OUNCES COCONUT WATER**

**.5 OUNCE CILANTRO-LIME SYRUP (SEE PAGE 111)**

**LIME SLICE, FOR GARNISH**

This drink could also be called a Tale of Two Genies. As a kid, I watched a lot of TV Land, so Barbara Eden was a frequent presence in my life. Then, obviously, there was the '90s genie in a bottle, Christina Aguilera. These were two genies I wish I could have bottled together. In this drink, the herbal notes in the gin play off the herbal and citrus notes of the cilantro-lime syrup, and the tropical notes from the coconut water round things out. What you get is a bright, alluring, and somewhat sweet drink. (As a bonus, coconut water helps rehydrate you, so this cocktail is basically health food.)

**METHOD:** Add the gin, coconut water, and cilantro-lime syrup to a shaker with ice. Shake well and strain into a coupe glass and garnish with the lime slice. If you happen to have a genie bottle, add a straw and use that—just make sure there are no genies in it first.

**?** Before Christina Aguilera reached superstardom with "Genie in a Bottle," she earned a second-place finish on *Star Search* as a nine-year-old in 1990 for her rendition of "A Sunday Kind of Love."

# I'M THE COCKTAIL, GOTTA LOVE ME

**2 OUNCES VODKA**

**.25 OUNCE HONEY SYRUP (SEE PAGE 110)**

**.5 OUNCE LEMON JUICE**

**CLUB SODA, TO FILL**

**ROSEMARY SPRIG**

It's hard to pick a favorite TGIF show, but *Dinosaurs* is up there. I remember uttering phrases like "Not the momma!" and "I'm the baby, gotta love me" frequently, much to the chagrin of my parents and sister. This cocktail was created for my partner one night when we only had a few ingredients in the house but still wanted a drink to kick back and relax with. The club soda and lemon provide a nice zesty boost while the honey syrup adds just a touch of sweetness, making for an easy-drinking sipper whenever you want it.

**METHOD:** Shake the vodka, honey syrup, and lemon juice with ice. Strain into a rocks glass filled with ice. Top with the club soda. Express the rosemary (slap it) like you're the baby and it is the father, Earl Sinclair, and use it to give the drink a quick stir to incorporate the club soda.

# HEY ARNOLD PALMER

**2 OUNCES SWEET TEA VODKA**

**1 OUNCE REPOSADO TEQUILA**

**4 OUNCES LEMONADE**

**LEMON WEDGE, FOR GARNISH**

Hey, Football Head! You don't have to put on a song and dance with your best friend while dressed as a banana to get a tasty flavor combination. Iced tea and lemonade, when mixed together, always make a great team. This cocktail is a twist on the classic drink, the Arnold Palmer (or John Daly, since we're using booze). Not only does this incorporate vodka but also a little bit of reposado tequila in order to play off the tannic flavors in the tea.

**METHOD:** Fill a Collins glass with ice. Add the vodka, tequila, and lemonade. Stir, and garnish with the lemon wedge. Yell, "Fore!" before every swig. (No one will think you're weird. Really.)

**?** The character of Arnold was originally created while Hey Arnold's creator, Craig Bartlett, was working on Pee-Wee's Playhouse. Arnold's distinctive head shape (as well as the other characters' shapes) was due to advice given to Bartlett by The Simpsons creator, Matt Groening, who told Bartlett to make characters you could recognize in silhouette.

# THE RYE-U AND KEN

**2 OUNCES RYE WHISKEY**

**.75 OUNCE SWEET VERMOUTH**

**ORANGE BITTERS**

**CHERRY, FOR GARNISH**

It's pretty amazing how much entertainment you can get from battling it out using only a few different characters (or just one if you were the person who always picked the same player no matter what) on just a handful of static backdrops. Personally, in *Street Fighter*, I was a Ken guy (followed by Guile, Sagat, and Chun-Li), but I knew plenty of friends who'd choose Ryu every time. Like a Hadoken for your taste buds, this cocktail is a classic move.

**METHOD:** Add the whiskey, vermouth, and bitters to a mixing glass. Stir with ice and strain into a old-fashioned glass. Garnish with the cherry.

# THE BURDEN OF 90 PROOF

**2 OUNCES BOURBON (90 PROOF, OBVIOUSLY)**

**.25 OUNCE AMARETTO**

**.5 OUNCE GINGER SYRUP (SEE PAGE 112)**

**CLUB SODA, TO FILL**

**LIME WEDGE, FOR GARNISH**

I wasn't watching thrillers as a child, but I did love watching a lot of movie trailers. There was just something about the epic music, the (what I would learn was) sexual intrigue, and of course, the murder. The theatrical trailer for Scott Turow's novel-turned-movie *The Burden of Proof* had all of that (plus ample amounts of slow motion and fog). This drink is a nod to all of those thriller trailers—a little sensuality from the amaretto, a bit of spice from the ginger syrup, and of course, the strong lead that comes from the bourbon. Have one or two of these and you'll think you can solve crimes.

**METHOD:** Add ice to an old-fashioned glass. Shake the bourbon, amaretto, and ginger syrup together with ice. Strain into the glass and top with the club soda. Garnish with the lime wedge.

**TIP:** Don't want to make ginger syrup? Use ginger ale in place of the ginger syrup and club soda (just don't add it before shaking because then the burden of proof will be all over your face).

# BLUE DA BA DEE DA BA DYED

**1.5 OUNCES BLUE CURAÇAO**

**1.5 OUNCES WHITE RUM**

**1 OUNCE COCONUT RUM**

**3 OUNCES PINEAPPLE JUICE**

**1 OUNCE LIME JUICE**

There've been many songs over the decades that are all but unintelligible at times. There was "Louie Louie," "In-A-Gadda-Da-Vida," and "Rock the Casbah." Eiffel 65 were no Clash (not even close), but "Blue (Da Ba Dee)" was my "Rock the Casbah." I remember getting into fierce elementary school debates over this song and its proper lyrics. This drink revolves, obviously, around the blue curaçao. Add to that the tropical flavors of white and coconut rums, as well as pineapple and lime juices, and you, too, can see blue wherever you go.

**METHOD:** Shake all of the ingredients together with ice. Strain into a (blue) hurricane glass filled with (blue) crushed ice.

**TIP:** To make blue crushed ice, simply add a few drops of blue food dye to the cubes before you freeze them. If you're going to garnish this one, you better make sure you've stocked up on blue items. Some options might be: blueberries, blue Fruit by the Foot, and blue umbrellas.

# DELIGHTFUL ORANGE DRINK

**2.5 OUNCES VODKA**

**3 OUNCES TANGERINE JUICE**

**2 OUNCES PEACH PUREE**

**1.5 OUNCES PEAR JUICE**

Of all the iconic commercials from the '90s, the one that sticks with me the most is the SunnyD commercial—the "purple stuff" one. Seriously, if you go back and watch, that mother buys what seems like a case of the stuff. How much SunnyD were her kid and his friends drinking? It was good, but it wasn't that good. This version, though, I'd buy by the case.

**METHOD:** Add all of the ingredients to a shaker with ice. Shake and strain into a Collins glass filled with ice.

**TIP:** If you can't find tangerine juice, orange juice will work in a pinch.

# CLEARLY CITRUS

**1 OUNCE VODKA**

**1 OUNCE LEMON-FLAVORED VODKA**

**.25 OUNCE ORANGE-FLAVORED RUM**

**.25 OUNCE LIME JUICE**

**.5 OUNCE SIMPLE SYRUP (SEE PAGE 110)**

**SODA, TO FILL**

I never got to taste Zima in the '90s, but I knew, thanks to my glorious overlord—television—that it was the cool thing to drink. Here, I've played with the citrus flavors that Zima says it contains and mixed up the types of liquors a little bit. It won't be clear like the original Zima because of the lime juice, but you will still get a range of sweet and tangy fruit flavors from the lemon vodka, orange rum, and lime juice.

**METHOD:** Add the vodkas, rum, lime juice, and simple syrup to a shaker. Shake well with ice and strain into a Collins glass. Top with the soda and stir to incorporate.

**TIP:** Up your Zima game by dropping a Jolly Rancher into the bottom of the glass before you pour the cocktail in.

# BOX OF CHOCOLATE

**1 OUNCE VAN GOGH DUTCH CHOCOLATE VODKA**

**1 OUNCE VODKA**

**1 OUNCE SKIM MILK**

**.25 OUNCE VANILLA SYRUP (SEE PAGE 111)**

**.25 OUNCE CHOCOLATE SYRUP**

**3 DASHES OF CHOCOLATE BITTERS**

For at least half of my elementary school career, I had peanut butter and jelly for lunch. Paired with that, if it wasn't a box of Ssips, it was Yoo-hoo (you could say I had a thing for sugary drinks, but any kid who drank anything in the '90s had the same thing). The fake chocolate flavor complemented the sandwich perfectly. This drink is a version of the uncomplicated joy of Yoo-hoo, invoking the chocolaty sugar rush of the playground.

**METHOD:** Place all of the ingredients in a shaker with ice and shake well, about twenty seconds. Pour into a martini glass and serve up.

**TIP:** If you want to go full '90s, search out a Tupperware martini glass and serve it in that.

# GHOST-BUSTING JUICE

**1.5 OUNCES VODKA**

**.5 OUNCE WHITE RUM**

**.25 OUNCE BLUE CURAÇAO**

**1 OUNCE ORANGE JUICE**

**.5 OUNCE TANGERINE JUICE**

**.25 OUNCE LEMON JUICE**

**.25 OUNCE LIME JUICE**

**A DROP OR TWO OF GREEN FOOD COLORING**

**LIME SLICE, FOR GARNISH**

When it comes to juice boxes, Hi-C Ecto Cooler—a tie-in product from *Ghostbusters II* and featuring the lovable (in the cartoons, yet not in the movies) accomplice Slimer— stands out above most in my mind. It was the drink you got during snack time at summer camp, the one that was what you begged your mother to get at the grocery store because it had a character you recognized on it. Greenish in color, thanks to the food dyes that *might* eventually kill us, it was supposed to be orange-tangerine flavored. They may have stopped making Hi-C Ecto Cooler in the early aughts, but it will always live on in our hearts.

**METHOD:** Mix the vodka, rum, curaçao, juices, and food coloring together and shake. Play with the proportion of the curaçao to get your perfect green color. Strain into a Collins glass with ice. To make it a little more Slimer-y, put everything into a blender and make it into a frozen drink! Garnish with the lime slice.

# ALOHA PUNCH

2 STRAWBERRIES

4 RASPBERRIES

2 OUNCES WHITE
RUM

1 OUNCE PINEAPPLE
JUICE

1 OUNCE
SIMPLE SYRUP
(SEE PAGE 110)

.75 OUNCE ORANGE
JUICE

.25 OUNCE LEMON
JUICE

.25 OUNCE LIME
JUICE

Hawaiian Punch was the ideal birthday party drink. Not only did it come in those funky little square boxes (or in the giant cans that had to be opened with a can opener), but it went perfectly with pizza. The go-to was red, but the blue flavor was a close second. It also inspired the schoolyard prank of asking someone if they wanted a Hawaiian Punch and, when they said yes, punching them. Kids can be so cruel (though, to be fair, if you thought your friend was going to magically produce a box of Hawaiian Punch on the schoolyard, you might have deserved it).

**METHOD:** In a cocktail shaker, muddle one of the strawberries (setting aside the other for garnish) and all of the raspberries. Add the rest of the ingredients and shake well. Double strain into a rocks glass filled with ice. Garnish with the remaining strawberry.

The original formula for Hawaiian Punch was developed in 1934 as an ice cream topping.

# THE Y2K

**1 OUNCE BOURBON**

**1 OUNCE DARK RUM**

**1 OUNCE AÑEJO TEQUILA**

**1 OUNCE SWEET RED VERMOUTH**

**.5 OUNCE AMARO (SUCH AS MONTENEGRO)**

**ORANGE ZEST, FOR GARNISH**

**MARASCHINO CHERRY, FOR GARNISH**

We've made it. The end of the decade. When midnight hit on January 1, 2000, I went over to look at our computer. Had it sprouted legs and become sentient? Had it died? Well, no. It kept on doing what it was doing, as we all did. This cocktail is like the lead-up to Y2K—dark, mysterious, and possibly even capable of resetting the world (or getting you drunk and having you pass out—basically the same thing). Sip this one, and remember 1999, when we thought the computers might win.

**METHOD:** Stir the bourbon, rum, tequila, vermouth, and amaro with ice and strain into a double rocks glass with a large cube in it. Garnish with the orange zest and maraschino cherry.

# APPENDICES

## SYRUPS

For some of the cocktails, you're going to need to make syrups. Syrups obviously sweeten and, when they are infused, add another layer of flavor to your drink with very little effort.

For all these, make sure to let the syrup cool before using. Stored in a glass jar in the fridge, a syrup should last about a month.

## SIMPLE SYRUP

**1 CUP WHITE SUGAR**
**1 CUP WATER**

**METHOD:** Add the sugar and water to a saucepan. Bring to a boil and stir until the sugar has dissolved.

**EXTRA:** There are as many simple syrup recipes out there as there are bartenders. You can switch up the flavor profile by playing around with the type of sugar (demerara, anyone?) and the ratio of sugar to water.

## HONEY SYRUP

**1 CUP WATER**
**1 CUP WILDFLOWER HONEY**
**(OR A LOCAL HONEY OF YOUR CHOICE)**

**METHOD:** Add the water and honey to a saucepan and bring to a boil. Reduce heat to low and stir until the honey dissolves. Allow to cool.

# CINNAMON SYRUP

**1 CUP SUGAR**
**1 CUP WATER**
**6 TO 8 CINNAMON STICKS**

**METHOD:** Add the sugar and water to a saucepan. Bring to a boil and stir until the sugar has dissolved. Add the cinnamon sticks and store in the fridge overnight. The next day, take out the cinnamon sticks and store.

# CILANTRO-LIME SYRUP

**1 CUP SUGAR**
**1 CUP WATER**
**.5 CUP CHOPPED CILANTRO**
**.25 CUP LIME JUICE**
**1 TABLESPOON LIME ZEST**

**METHOD:** Add the sugar and water to a saucepan. Bring to a boil and stir until the sugar has dissolved. Stir in the cilantro, lime juice, and lime zest. Allow to cool, then strain.

# VANILLA SYRUP

**1 CUP SUGAR**
**1 VANILLA BEAN, SPLIT IN HALF**
**1 CUP WATER**

**METHOD:** Add the sugar, split vanilla bean, and water to a saucepan. Bring to a boil and stir until the sugar has dissolved. Strain out the vanilla and cool.

# GINGER SYRUP

**1 CUP SUGAR**
**1 CUP WATER**
**4 OUNCES FRESH GINGER ROOT**

**METHOD:** Add the sugar and water to a saucepan. Bring to a boil and stir until the sugar has dissolved. Peel the ginger and cut it into small coins. Add the coins to the mixture and bring the pot to a simmer. Remove from the heat. Let the syrup cool for a half hour, then strain.

# INFUSIONS

Another way to add flavor to cocktails is to infuse the spirits themselves. Infusions are pretty easy to accomplish—in short, it is a lot of hurry up and wait. Below you will find the infusions that are used in this book.

# BLACK PEPPER-INFUSED WHISKEY

**2 TABLESPOONS CRACKED**
**PEPPERCORNS (I GO WITH BLACK,**
**BUT FEEL FREE TO MIX IT UP A LITTLE)**

**1 BOTTLE TENNESSEE WHISKEY**

**METHOD:** Add peppercorns and whiskey to a clean mason jar. Seal and store for a week. Strain liquid into a sterilized glass container (like another mason jar).

# LAVENDER-INFUSED GIN

**2 TEASPOONS DRIED LAVENDER OR 4 SPRIGS FRESH LAVENDER**

**1 BOTTLE DRY GIN**

**METHOD:** Add the lavender and gin to a clean mason jar. Seal and store for two days. Strain liquid into a sterilized glass container (like another mason jar).

# PREPARING TO GET JIGGY WIT IT

With so many '90s cocktails now at your disposal, it only makes sense that you must throw the rager of last century with them. Mix up a few of these drinks for people who are dressed like they just walked off the set of *White Men Can't Jump* and pump up the jams.

## THE ULTIMATE '90S PLAYLISTS

As the evil brother of a famous African king once said, be prepared. You can't have a '90s party without '90s music. It's just not right. If nothing else, you'll run out of booze, as no one will have anything to do *but* drink.

Depending on what sort of party you're hosting, and what the crowd you've invited is like (you don't want to give anyone flashbacks of their debilitating crush caused by the mere mention of JT's tightly curled locks), you'll need to tailor your playlist. Here, you'll find a few samples to get you going. Put these playlists on, and pretty soon everyone will be using their Solo cups as microphones and making the most epic moves the world has ever seen.

Don't feel like tracking these playlists down? I've gone ahead and put them on Spotify. Simply search for "Are You Afraid of the Dark Rum?: [Playlist Title]" on Spotify, queue them up, hit Shuffle Play, and you're ready to party like it's 1999.

# BOY BANDS AND GIRL GROUPS

5ive—"When the Lights Go Out"
Backstreet Boys—"Quit Playing Games (with My Heart)"
Backstreet Boys—"Everybody (Backstreet's Back)"
Backstreet Boys—"As Long as You Love Me"
Backstreet Boys—"I Want It That Way"
98 Degrees—"I Do (Cherish You)"
98 Degrees—"Invisible Man"
soulDecision—"Faded"
LFO—"Summer Girls"
Hanson—"MMMBop"
New Kids on the Block—"Step by Step"
New Kids on the Block—"If You Go Away"
*NSYNC—"I Want You Back"
*NSYNC —"Tearin' Up My Heart"
Take That—"Back for Good"
BBMak—"Back Here"
Westlife—"Swear It again"
Westlife—"If I Let You Go"

Spice Girls—"Wannabe"
Spice Girls—"Spice Up Your Life"
Blaque—"Bring It All to Me"
En Vogue—"My Lovin' (You're Never Gonna Get It)"
B*Witched—"C'est la Vie"
All Saints—"If You Wanna Party (I Found Lovin')"
All Saints—"Never Ever"
TLC—"Creep"
TLC—"Waterfalls"
TLC—"No Scrubs"
Destiny's Child—"Bills, Bills, Bills"
Destiny's Child—"Say My Name"
Cleopatra—"Cleopatra's Theme"

# ROCK AND POP

Third Eye Blind—"Semi-Charmed Life"
Lit—"My Own Worst Enemy"
Nirvana—"Smells Like Teen Spirit"
Whitney Houston—"I Will Always Love You"
Ricky Martin—"Livin' la Vida Loca"
Smashmouth—"All Star"
Christina Aguilera—"Genie in a Bottle"
Britney Spears—"Baby One More Time"
Beck—"Loser"
Ace of Base—"The Sign"
Wilson Phillips—"Hold On"
Extreme—"More Than Words"
Michael Jackson—"Black or White"
Will Smith—"Gettin' Jiggy wit It"

Toni Braxton—"Unbreak My Heart"
Quad City DJ's—"Space Jam"
Cher—"Believe"
Aerosmith—"I Don't Want to Miss a Thing"
Enrique Iglesias—"Bailamos"
Santana ft. Rob Thomas—"Smooth"
Madonna—"Vogue"
Counting Crows—"Mr. Jones"
Duncan Sheik—"Barely Breathing"
Blink-182—"What's My Age Again?"
Green Day—"Basket Case"
Evan and Jaron—"Crazy for This Girl"
Blessid Union of Souls—"Hey Leonardo (She Likes Me for Me)"
Goo Goo Dolls—"Iris"
The Cardigans—"Lovefool"
Mighty Mighty Bosstones—"The Impression That I Get"

# R&B, RAP, AND HIP HOP

Boyz II Men—"End of the Road"
Boyz II Men—"I'll Make Love to You"
Blackstreet—"No Diggity"
All-4-One—"I Swear"
New Edition—"Hit Me Off"
Coolio—"Gangsta's Paradise"
2Pac—"California Love"
MC Hammer—"U Can't Touch This"
Sir Mix-a-Lot—"Baby Got Back"
Dr. Dre—"Nuthin but a G Thang"
Vanilla Ice—"Ice, Ice Baby"

Color Me Badd—"I Adore Mi Amor"
Color Me Badd—"I Wanna Sex You Up"
Kris Kross—"Jump"
R. Kelly—"Bump n' Grind"
Montell Jordan—"This Is How We Do It"
Lauryn Hill—"Doo Wop (That Thing)"
Bone Thugs N Harmony—"Tha Crossroads"
The Notorious B.I.G.—"Hyponotize"
Puff Daddy—"I'll Be Missing You"
Naughty by Nature—"Hip Hip Hooray"
Wu-Tang Clan—"C.R.E.A.M."
Salt-n-Pepa—"Let's Talk About Sex"
Bell Biv DeVoe—"Poison"
A Tribe Called Quest—"Can I Kick It?"
OutKast—"Rosa Parks"
Beastie Boys—"Sabotage"
Ice Cube—"Check Yo Self"
Mya ft. ODB—"Ghetto Superstar"
Wyclef Jean—"Gone till November"

# ONE-HIT WONDERS*

OMC—"How Bizarre"
Technotronic—"Pump Up the Jam"
Eagle-Eye Cherry—"Save Tonight"
Natalie Imbruglia—"Torn"
Deep Blue Something—"Breakfast at Tiffany's"
Len—"Steal My Sunshine"
Marcy Playground—"Sex and Candy"
House of Pain—"Jump Around"

Haddaway—"What Is Love"
Chumbawamba—"Tubthumping"
Harvey Danger—"Flagpole Sitta"
The Verve—"Bitter Sweet Symphony"
Right Said Fred—"I'm Too Sexy"
Lou Bega—"Mambo No. 5"
Snow—"Informer"
Lisa Loeb—"Stay (I Missed You)"
Ini Kamoze—"Here Comes the Hotstepper"
Los del Rio—"Macarena"
Semisonic—"Closing Time"
Divinyls—"I Touch Myself"
Wreckx-N-Effect—"Rump Shaker"
4 Non Blondes—"What's Up?"
Us3—"Cantaloop (Flip Fantasia)"
Corona—"The Rhythm of the Night"
Rednex—"Cotton Eye Joe"
DJ Kool—"Let Me Clear My Throat"
Meredith Brooks—"Bitch"
Jennifer Paige—"Crush"
Big Mountain—"Baby, I Love Your Way"
Des'ree—"You Gotta Be"

*This playlist could have gone on for days. There are literally too many
one-hit wonders to choose from.*

# '90s DRINKING GAMES

Who doesn't like a good drinking game? These three games are flexible enough for whatever situation you've got going on at your party. Use these in conjunction with beer pong or other classic party drinking games to spice up your life (and the party)!

## WAZZUP WITH THAT DRINK?

Watch a '90s movie. Every time a character uses a phrase that was exclusively used in the '90s, take a drink. Don't want to do phrases? Try clothing! Every time a pair of parachute pants pops up, take a swig. Overalls with the straps down? That's two drinks right there.

## QUOTE OFF

Pick a popular (and quotable movie)—*Robin Hood: Men in Tights*, say. Take turns saying quotes from the movie. First person to mess up has to drink.

## TWISTER

A classic game already, but with more booze. Assign a certain number of drinks (sips) to each color, so that not only do you have to twist yourself into a pretzel but you also have to take a certain number of drinks depending on what color you get.

# ACKNOWLEDGMENTS

Just like the '90s, this book would not have become this awesome without a ton of people.

Eric Smith, you believed in this when it was just a series of text messages that I sent to you on a Friday night, fueled by the '90s Smash Hits playlist on Spotify. I can't thank you enough for thinking it should be out in the world.

Allison Adler, you took what I had and made it better than I ever could've, like Splinter did with the Teenage Mutant Ninja Turtles.

The people who supported me and offered advice through the process: Alan and Michelle Slaughter, Katie and Tom Hickey, Tina Slaughter, Nick Sweeney, Kenny Lane, Molly McGowan Gorsuch and Jamie Gorsuch, Cator Sparks, Robert Haynes Peterson, Katherine Spangler, Erin Elizabeth Smith, Joe Minarick, Emily Capettini, Jennie Frost, Victoria Dotson, Greg Dotson, Matt Mossman, Mike and Sharon Ellis, and Josh and Dorothy Williams.

The official Instagram of 98 Degrees, for liking a photo of me and my fake boy band mates (Clay Whittaker and Ethan Fixell) and making me believe anything is possible.

*The Manual/Digital Trends* staff, the bartenders, brand ambassadors, PR people, and other spirits-industry folks that I talked to about this, incessantly—you know who you are. From bus rides on press trips to hours-long tastings getting to indulge in the finer things in life, your drinks, your products, and your words all helped throughout the process.

Finally, Amy Ellis. You had to put up with every fact, dumb pun, and bad drink recipe that didn't make it into the book. You are the K-Ci to my JoJo, the Eiffel to my 65. There are no words to actually convey the amount of thanks I owe you for all that (the jokes aren't going to stop, though, just know that). I love you.

# INDEX

Aloha Punch, 106–7
amaretto, 94–95
amaro, 54–55, 108–9
Ancho Reyes (original), 50–51
Ancho Reyes Verde, 44–45
Angostura bitters, 18, 42–43
aperol, 68–69
apple slices, 46–47
Appleton Estate Rum, 62–63
Are You Afraid of the Dark Rum?, 26–27
As Long as You Rum Me, 66–67
The A/S/L, 68–69

Baby, I Love Your Wray, 62–63
Baby Got Black Label, 42–43
bar stock, 17–18
barspoon, 12
basil, 82–83
Bayou Spiced Rum, 50–51
beer, 28–29
bitters
 Angostura, 18, 42–43
 chocolate, 102–3

lavender, 70–71
orange, 18, 24–25, 54–55, 64–65, 92–93
rhubarb, 66–67
vanilla, 80–81
walnut, 26–27
yuzu, 60–61
Black Pepper-Infused Whiskey, 34–35, 112
blanco tequila, 30–31, 78–79, 84–85
blue curaçao
 Blue Da Ba Dee Da Ba Dyed, 96–97
 Ghost-Busting Juice, 104–5
Blue Da Ba Dee Da Ba Dyed, 96–97
blueberries, 46–47
Bombay Sapphire Gin, 22–23
bottle opener, 13
bourbon, 18
 The Burden of 90 Proof, 94–95
 Juice Box Iced Tea, 24–25
 Nothin' But a Mead Thing, 80–81
 The Y2K, 108–9
Box of Chocolate, 102–3

boy bands playlists, 114–15
brandy, 18
 cherry, 58–59
 I Saw the Wine, 46–47
British Lager, 28–29
The Burden of 90 Proof, 94–95

Campari, 74–75
Champagne, brut, 70–71
cherry brandy, 58–59
Cherry Heering
 Are You Afraid of the Dark Rum?, 26–27
 Nothin' But a Mead Thing, 80–81
chocolate-flavored drinks
 Box of Chocolate, 102–103
 Crème Rules Everything Around Me, 52–53
 The Mud Dog, 50–51
cider, dry, 28–29
Cilantro-Lime Syrup, 86–87, 111
Cinnamon Syrup, 66–67, 111
Clearly Citrus, 100–101
coconut, cream of, 72–73
coconut rum, 96–97

coconut sparkling water, 64–65
coconut water, 86–87
cognac, 58–59
crème de cacao
    Crème Rules Everything Around Me, 52–53
crème de cassis, 54–55
Crème Rules Everything Around Me, 52–53
Cynar, 40–41

Delightful Orange Drink, 98–99
difficulty, of mixing drinks, 19
Dolin Rouge, 38–39
drinking games, 119

egg white, 42–43

Fernet-Branca
    Fernetscape Navigator, 38–39
Fernetscape Navigator, 38–39
French 75, 70
The Fresh Mint of Bel-Air, 22–23

games, 119

Ghost-Busting Juice, 104–5
gin, 18
    The Fresh Mint of Bel-Air, 22–23
    The Gin Red Line, 74–75
    Ginny in a Bottle, 86–87
    Kimmy Gimlet, 36–37
    Lavender-Infused Gin, 36–37, 113
    Wicked Good Basil Cocktail, 82–83
    Windows 75, 70–71
The Gin Red Line, 74–75
Ginger Syrup, 94–95, 112
Ginny in a Bottle, 86–87
girl groups playlists, 114–15
glassware, 14–15
Glen Moray Chardonnay Cask Finish Scotch Whisky, 60–61
Grand Marnier, 38–39
grapefruit juice
    As Long as You Rum Me, 66–67
    Pop Culture, 78–79
grenadine, 30–31
grog, 48–49
guava nectar, 32–33

Hey Arnold Palmer, 90–91
hibiscus tea, 58–59
hip-hop playlists, 116–17
honey
    Honey Syrup, 88–89, 110
    Pop Culture, 78–79
hot chocolate, 50–51
hot drinks, 15
    I'm Too Sexy for This Grog, 48–49
    The Mud Dog, 50–51
House of Painkiller, 72–73

I Saw the Wine, 46–47
I'll Never Let Yuzu Go, Jack, 60–61
I'm the Cocktail, Gotta Love Me, 88–89
I'm Too Sexy for This Grog, 48–49
infusions
    Black Pepper-Infused Whiskey, 34–35, 112
    Lavender-Infused Gin, 36–37, 113
Irish whiskey, 18

Nothing Compares 2 D.E.W., 54–55
The Tubthumper, 28–29

Jägerbomberman, 44
Jägerbomberman 64, 45
Jägermeister
  Jägerbomberman, 44
  Jägerbomberman 64, 45
Jell-O shots, 84–85
jigger, 11–12
Johnnie Walker Black Label, 42–43
Juice Box Iced Tea, 24–25
juicer, 13

The Kelly Kapowski, 84–85
Kimmy Gimlet, 36–37
knife, 14

lavender
  bitters, 70–71
  Lavender-Infused Gin, 36–37, 113
lemon juice
  Baby Got Black Label, 42–43
  I'm the Cocktail, Gotta Love Me, 88–89
  Red Room Punch, 58–59
  Windows 75, 70–71

lemonade, 90–91
lemon-flavored vodka, 100–101
lime juice
  Cilantro-Lime Syrup, 86–87, 111
  Clearly Citrus, 100–101
  The Fresh Mint of Bel-Air, 22–23
  I Saw the Wine, 46–47
  I'm Too Sexy for This Grog, 48–49
  Kimmy Gimlet, 36–37
  Red Room Punch, 58–59
limoncello, 24–25
liqueurs, 18
  amaretto, 94–95
  amaro, 54–55, 108–9
  Ancho Reyes (chile), 44–45, 50–51
  Cherry Heering, 26–27, 80–81
  crème de cacao, 52–53
  crème de cassis, 54–55
  Grand Marnier, 38–39
  limoncello, 24–25
  maraschino, 68–69
  Triple Sec, 46–47
Livin' La Vida Coco, 64–65

Mambo No. 5, 30–31
maraschino liqueur, 68–69

mead, 64–65
  spiced, 80–81
metric conversions, 17
mezcal, 76–77
milk, 102–3
mint
  The Fresh Mint of Bel-Air, 22–23
  Semi-Charmed Kind of Cocktail, 56–57
mixing techniques, 16
molasses, 48–49
Montenegro, 54–55
moonshine, 84–85
movies, 1990s
  drinking games around, 119
  nostalgia, 50, 61, 62, 74, 94, 105
  trivia, 60
The Mud Dog, 50–51
music, 1990s
  nostalgia, 43, 57, 65, 66, 73
  playlists, 113–18
  trivia, 31, 42, 47, 52, 71, 87

Nothin' But a Mead Thing, 80–81
Nothing Compares 2 D.E.W., 54–55

one-hit wonders
  playlist, 117–18

orange bitters, 18
  Juice Box Iced Tea,
    24–25
  Livin' La Vida Coco,
    64–65
  Nothing Compares
    2 D.E.W., 54–55
  The Rye-U and Ken,
    92–93
orange juice
  Aloha Punch, 106–7
  Ghost-Busting Juice,
    104–5
  House of Painkiller,
    72–73
  Mambo No. 5, 30–31
  The POG, 32–33
orange rum
  Clearly Citrus,
    100–101
  The Zack Morris,
    84–85
orgeat, 62–63

peach puree, 98–99
pear juice, 98–99
pickle juice
  Pickleodeon, 34–35
  Slimy Mary, 40–41
Pickleodeon, 34–35
pineapple juice
  Aloha Punch, 106–7
  Baby, I Love Your
    Wray, 62–63

Blue Da Ba Dee Da
  Ba Dyed, 96–97
House of Painkiller,
  72–73
Jägerbomberman 64,
  45
Mambo No. 5, 30–31
The POG, 32–33
Wicked Good Basil
  Cocktail, 82–83
The POG, 32
pomegranate juice,
  56–57
Pop Culture, 78–79
pop music playlists,
  115–16
Pop Rocks
  Pop Culture, 78–79
  The Principal Belding,
    84–85
The Principal Belding,
  84–85
Prosecco, 22–23

Quote Off (game), 119

rap playlists, 116–17
raspberries, 106–7
raspberry vodka, 84–85
R&B playlists, 116–17
Red Room Punch, 58–59
red wine, 46–47
reposado tequila, 52–53,
  90–91
rhubarb bitters, 66–67

rock music playlists,
  115–16
The Rossi & Rachel,
  76–77
rum
  aged, 66–67
  Baby, I Love Your
    Wray, 62–63
  coconut, 96–97
  orange, 84–85,
    100–101
  Red Room Punch,
    58–59
  The Zack Morris
    (Jell-O shot), 84–85
rum, dark, 18
  Are You Afraid of the
    Dark Rum?, 26–27
  House of Painkiller,
    72–73
  I'm Too Sexy for This
    Grog, 48–49
  Mambo No. 5, 30–31
  The Y2K, 108–9
rum, light/white, 18
  Aloha Punch, 106–7
  Blue Da Ba Dee Da Ba
    Dyed, 96–97
  Ghost-Busting Juice,
    104–5
  Mambo No. 5, 30–31
  The POG, 32
  Semi-Charmed Kind
    of Cocktail, 56–57
  The Slammer, 33

rum, overproof
  Baby, I Love Your
    Wray, 62–63
  Mambo No. 5, 30–31
  The POG, 32–33
rum, spiced
  Are You Afraid of the
    Dark Rum?, 26–27
  Livin' La Vida Coco,
    64–65
  The Mud Dog, 50–51
rye whiskey, 18
  The Rye-U and Ken,
    92–93
The Rye-U and Ken,
    92–93

Sailor Jerry Spiced Rum,
    26–27
Saved by the Jell-O,
    84–85
Scotch whisky, 18
  The A/S/L, 68–69
  Fernetscape Navigator,
    38–39
  I'll Never Let Yuzu Go,
    Jack, 60–61
The Screech, 84–85
seaweed, 40–41
Semi-Charmed Kind of
    Cocktail, 56–57
shakers, 12
shaking technique, 16
shopping list, 17–18
Simple Syrup, 110

The Slammer, 33
Slimy Mary, 40–41
smoke/smoke gun,
    26–27
spirits, stocking, 17–18
strainers, 13
strawberries
  Aloha Punch, 106–7
  The Fresh Mint of
    Bel-Air, 22–23
sweet tea vodka, 90–91
syrups
  chocolate, 102–3
  Cilantro-Lime Syrup,
    86–87, 111
  Cinnamon Syrup,
    66–67, 111
  Ginger Syrup, 94–95,
    112
  Honey Syrup, 88–89,
    110
  Simple Syrup, 110
  Vanilla Syrup, 102–3,
    111

tangerine juice
  Delightful Orange
    Drink, 98–99
  Ghost-Busting Juice,
    104–5
technology, 1990s, 39,
    69, 70–71
television, 1990s
  nostalgia, 9, 26, 35,
    36, 40, 58, 77, 89

trivia, 23, 59, 79, 90
tequila, 18
  Crème Rules Every-
    thing Around Me,
    52–53
  Hey Arnold Palmer,
    90–91
  Mambo No. 5, 30–31
  mezcal, 76–77
  Pop Culture, 78–79
  The Screech (Jell-O
    shot), 84–85
  The Y2K, 108–9
tomatoes, green, 40–41
tools, 11–14
Triple Sec, 46–47
The Tubthumper, 28–29
Tullamore D.E.W. Irish
    whiskey, 54–55
Twister (game), 119

van Gogh Dutch
    Chocolate Vodka,
    102–3
vanilla
  bitters, 80–81
  Vanilla Syrup, 102–3,
    111
vermouth
  sweet, 54–55,
    92–93
  sweet red, 74–75,
    76–77, 108–9
video games, 1990s,
    44, 93

vodka, 18
Box of Chocolate,
102–3
chocolate, 102–3
Clearly Citrus, 100–101
Crème Rules Every-
thing Around Me,
52–53
Delightful Orange
Drink, 98–99
Ghost-Busting Juice,
104–5
Hey Arnold Palmer,
90–91
I'm the Cocktail, Gotta
Love Me, 88–89
The Kelly Kapowski
(Jell-O shot), 84–85
lemon-flavored,
100–101
raspberry, 84–85
Slimy Mary, 40–41
sweet tea, 90–91
The Tubthumper,
28–29

walnut bitters, 26–27
Wazzup with that Drink?
(game), 119
whiskey. *See also* Irish
whiskey; Scotch
whisky
Baby Got Black Label,
42–43
Black Pepper-Infused,
34–35, 112

Pickleodeon, 34–35
The Principal Belding
(Jell-O shot), 84–85
rye, 18, 92–93
white, 84–85
Wicked Good Basil
Cocktail, 82–83
Windows 75, 70–71
wine, red, 46–47
Worcestershire sauce,
40–41
Wray & Nephew
Overproof Rum, 62–63

The Y2K, 108–9
yuzu bitters, 60–61

The Zack Morris, 84–85

Andrews McMeel Publishing
a division of Andrews McMeel Universal
1130 Walnut Street, Kansas City, Missouri 64106
www.andrewsmcmeel.com

19 20 21 22 23 TEN 10 9 8 7 6 5 4 3 2 1

ISBN: 978-1-4494-9156-7

Library of Congress Control Number: 2018958238

Photographer: Amy Ellis
Editor: Allison Adler
Art Director/Designer: Spencer Williams
Production Editor: Elizabeth A. Garcia
Production Manager: Carol Coe

**ATTENTION: SCHOOLS AND BUSINESSES**

Andrews McMeel books are available at quantity discounts with bulk purchase for educational, business, or sales promotional use. For information, please e-mail the Andrews McMeel Publishing Special Sales Department: specialsales@amuniversal.com.